A LITTLE KNOWLEDGE CAN GO A LONG WAY

toward making you the top trivia expert around. For example, did you know that:

- Cuffs on men's pants were first designed to hold cigar ashes.

- In 1659, Massachusetts outlawed Christmas.

- There are so many automobiles on the road today that the entire population of the United States could be accommodated in the front seats.

If you didn't know these facts, there's a good chance your friends won't, either. And with the over 1600 goodies included in this collection, you'll be able to amaze them again and again. It's fun. It's fascinating. It's a trivia lover's dream.

MIXED NUTS

Other SIGNET Books You'll Want to Read

If you wish to order these titles,
please see the coupon in
the back of this book.

MIXED NUTS

by
E. C. McKenzie

A SIGNET BOOK
NEW AMERICAN LIBRARY
TIMES MIRROR

SIGNET, SIGNET CLASSICS, MENTOR, PLUME AND MERIDIAN BOOKS
are published by The New American Library, Inc.,
1301 Avenue of the Americas, New York, New York 10019

FIRST SIGNET PRINTING, JUNE, 1978

1 2 3 4 5 6 7 8 9

MIXED NUTS

According to a recent estimate, there are more than sixteen million bed-wetters in the United States.

In Norfolk, Virginia, it is illegal for a girl to go to a public dance unless she wears a corset.

The top speed of a sneeze is about two hundred miles per hour.

Turkeys are prone to high blood pressure.

The women in Kadakh, India, comb their hair only once a year.

In 1924 horses were sold in Australia for one cent each.

There are four rows of whiskers on a cat's face.

Most snakes cannot survive being X rayed.

Abraham Lincoln's coffin was opened in 1887 and again in 1901 to make sure the body was still there.

A woodpecker can peck five hundred times per minute.

Women buy four out of every ten screwdrivers sold.

Elephants are always hungry.

The little town of Hatch, New Mexico, is known as "The Chili Capital of the World."

A flea jumps two hundred times the length of its own body, which is the equivalent of a six-foot man jumping five city blocks.

The temperature of a hen's body is about 107 degrees Fahrenheit.

Cuffs on men's pants were first designed to hold cigar ashes.

Many Russian women in the Caucasus Mountains still wear leather underwear.

Homing pigeons have three sets of eyelids.

The citizens of Barre, Vermont, are called upon by ordinance to take a bath every Saturday night.

Hindus always eat with their right hand and drink with their left.

A whale can swim for three months without eating.

Mexican-born Lucia Zarate was the smallest woman who ever lived. She was less than twenty inches tall and weighed five pounds.

Alligators drown if held under water.

The lawmakers in Pittsburgh have made it illegal to sleep in a refrigerator.

It is against U.S. Navy regulations for an officer to cheer at football games.

A newborn kangaroo is about the size of a bumblebee.

Catnappers invariably snore.

Prairie dogs and wild asses never drink water.

A baby born in 1928 in Knoxville, Tennessee, had a tail seven inches long.

Adolf Hitler once owned 8,960 acres of land in the state of Colorado.

Monkeys are extremely fond of kissing.

President James Buchanan was nearsighted in one eye and farsighted in the other.

Bees cannot fly in the rain.

Frogs prefer the color of blue. They'll jump toward blue every time.

As a hobby, Mrs. William Norton of England, collected glass eyeballs for many years.

Dolphins sleep with one eye open at all times.

Pearls will dissolve in strong vinegar.

There are no fish as intelligent as the octopus.

Daniel Webster rehearsed all of his speeches by speaking to a tree.

An onion placed in a newly painted room will soak up the odor of the paint.

The first bird domesticated by man was the goose.

A psychiatric clinic in Europe is treating five thousand mentally-ill dogs per year.

Drowning victims, when found, are always face down.

The Caspian Sea, between Europe and Asia, is the largest inland salt lake in the world.

Approximately 8 percent of the grownups in America need no more than five hours of sleep each night.

The baseball fan spends an average of $1.65 on food and drink in the ballpark.

A large number of children who undergo major surgery before the age of two later come down with asthma.

The eucalyptus trees of Australia are the tallest trees in the world—in rare instances reaching a height of four hundred feet.

The average American woman now has her last child at twenty-six.

One-half of the members of the Rodeo Cowboys Association have never worked a ranch.

The first United States coin to bear a president's portrait was the 1909 Lincoln penny.

If you poured all the ocean water into a plastic bag, it would be about one-third as large as the moon.

A newly-born guinea pig can shift for himself three days after birth.

Twenty-two out of every one hundred girls between the age of eighteen and nineteen are already married.

One hundred years ago, a woman thought herself to be particularly gifted if she were one of those who grew a faint mustache.

In 1659, Massachusetts outlawed Christmas. Anybody found observing Christmas in any way was fined five shillings.

Coffee sold for four dollars per pound in 1863 in Atlanta at the height of the Civil War.

Tulsa, Oklahoma, is the world's largest manufacturer of winches and industrial heaters.

The stethoscope was invented in 1837 by Dr. William Stokes, an Irish physician.

Women comprise 45 percent of the automobile drivers in the United States.

At the age of five, four out of five children are afraid of dogs.

About four thousand years ago the Chinese learned how to unravel silkworm cocoons and weave the silk into cloth.

Frogs have teeth; toads don't.

Chicago has the world's busiest mailbox. The box has to be emptied six times per day. Location: intersection of Madison and Halsted streets.

One out of every seven new husbands is younger than his bride.

A survey of 280 women revealed that only 11 of them had never received a marriage proposal.

It takes 4 million flowers to get two pounds of jasmine.

There are so many automobiles on the road today that the entire United States population could be accommodated in the front seats.

The original Greyhound Bus was a 1914, seven-passenger Hupmobile.

Tonsillectomy is no longer the most frequently performed surgery in the United States. Abortion is number one.

There are more than ten million tennis players in the United States.

The silk in a spider's web will stretch one-fifth of its length before breaking.

In Finland, it's expected that the bride cry throughout the wedding ceremony.

Herbert Hoover was the only president of the United States who left behind fewer federal employees at the White House than were there when he first took office.

The average American eats about two pounds of sugar per week, more than 70 percent of which is in processed foods.

People in England can now get a divorce by mail.

The Great Lakes are bigger in area than Pennsylvania and New York combined.

There are only two words in the English language that spell the same object both forward and backward. They are "race car."

Blond hair comes undone most quickly in the fog.

The first book ever printed in England was *The Game of Chess*.

Farm animals in the United States create about 2 billion tons of waste per year.

A thin film of glue makes a stronger joint than a thick film.

Colorblindness occurs in about 6.5 percent of men but in less than 1 percent of women.

A frog's eye won't register anything that doesn't move.

In its pure state, salt pours just as readily in damp weather as in dry. It is not so with table salt.

An announcer can get about fifty-eight words into a thirty-second TV commercial.

Fish accounts for 85 percent of Iceland's exports.

Sound does not travel through a vacuum.

Texas has more deer than any other state.

There are ninety-two different atoms found in nature, one for each of the ninety-two chemical elements.

The average automobile tire rotates more than thirty million times during its lifetime.

There are forty-one mountain peaks in Colorado more than fourteen thousand feet in altitude.

Stutterers don't stutter when they whisper.

Bees normally concentrate on collecting the nectar of only one kind of flower at a time.

The tapeworm is a parasite that has neither mouth nor stomach. It "soaks up" food through the skin.

A protective material covers the scales of live fish, and if this cover is removed by improper handling, the fish may die.

Alcohol feels cooler to the touch than water because it evaporates at a much faster rate at body temperature.

Doubling the diameter of a pipe increases its capacity four times.

One pound of air measures 12.4 cubic feet.

On March 18, 1931, the first electric razor was placed on sale.

There are only thirteen manufacturers of artificial eyes in the United States.

Mark Twain's great novel *Tom Sawyer* was the first typed manuscript ever submitted by an American author—in 1875.

A newly hatched crocodile is three times as long as the egg from which it emerged.

In a small town in India, everybody attends the wedding—except the bride's mother.

The United States now has approximately as many horses as college students.

DDT, the first man-made insecticide, was first marketed in 1944.

When a person rides an elevator downward, his weight is almost 10 percent less than when stationary.

A good swimmer can reach a speed of about four miles per hour for a short distance.

The Washington Monument sways only one-eighth of an inch in a thirty-mile-per-hour wind. It has settled only two inches in thirty years.

A fish would have no trouble seeing objects when it is out of water.

The seismograph was developed in 1855 to record the shock waves produced by earthquakes.

In 1822, an English experimenter by the name of James Perkins built the first steam rocket.

A plastic surgeon in New York City makes most of his money by cutting dimples in cheeks and chins.

The top speed of a man is about twenty-two miles per hour.

Wilson Bentley, a farmer near Jericho, Vermont, was the first to measure the size of raindrops.

It is easier to converse over music than over other kinds of voices or noises.

The Chinese goose often lays as many as thirty eggs at a time.

Most scientists define a desert as a place having less than ten inches of rain each year, as compared with fifty inches for a relatively moist region.

It is actually not the adult moth that damages clothing, but rather the offspring of the moth, called *larvae*.

A one-inch cube of cork contains about 200 million air-filled cells.

The thrush is perhaps the most gifted of the singing birds.

A gallon of cool air at sea level weighs about one-fifth of an ounce.

Today, short-range weather forecasts are 80 percent accurate.

In 1962, a former checkers champion lost a game for the first time in eight years. His opponent was an IBM Model 7094 electronic computer.

A cat can see six times better than a human being.

Honeybees are deaf.

It's the custom in Iceland to test modesty by tickling.

No man has ever been elected president of the

United States who did not have a Christian background.

The gum on the back of a postage stamp contains about one-tenth of a calorie.

Cataplexy is a condition that paralyzes its victims after strong emotional stimulus.

Certain fish will die from lack of air if they are held under water and are not permitted to come to the surface to breathe.

Mourners in Japan wear white.

The male mosquito cannot bite a person, no matter how hard he tries.

More onion sets are grown in Michigan than in any other state.

A black sheep has a much sharper sense of smell than a white sheep.

A late report discloses that Winston Churchill smoked more than three hundred thousand cigars during his lifetime.

Mountain people have a larger heart than valley people, and blood that is richer in cells.

According to a medical specialist, the best way to lose weight is to curb the appetite by eating an apple half an hour before every meal.

Seventy-two muscles are used in speaking one word.

Soccer is played in more countries than any other sport.

Salt Island, one of the British Virgin Islands, has a population of eight.

Land surveys in the delta region of the Mississippi River show that the surface is sinking about eight feet per century.

The earth is about twenty-seven miles thicker at the equator than through the poles.

British scholars have found that people who wear eyeglasses generally are more intelligent than those who don't wear them.

A team of surgeons in Shanghai have reattached 100 severed hands with an 85 percent success rate.

In Arkansas it's against the law to drive blindfolded cattle on public roads.

Elias Howe's toughest problem in his attempt to invent the sewing machine was where to put the eye of the needle. This problem delayed him for months.

Martha Washington's bathing suit looked somewhat like a nightgown—with elbow-length sleeves, a high neck, and lead weights sewn into the hems at the ankles.

Turtles are deaf.

Mormons must keep a year's supply of food on hand for emergencies.

Before 1850, virtually all the women in the United States wore plain, drab underwear.

A cat purrs while exhaling and inhaling. One vocal cord vibrates during inhalation, the other during exhalation.

Synthetic rubber now accounts for three-fourths of the United States' rubber production, and for one-third of all rubber used in the world.

In 1926, a blue whale was weighed, piece by piece, and its total weight added up to a staggering 135 tons.

Cicero once thought he had a cure for the familiar "hangover." He said cabbage would do the trick—but he was mistaken.

Among those husbands who engage in an extramarital affair, only one in ten divorces his wife to marry the new-found object of his affections.

President Calvin Coolidge is credited with writing a history of the United States in five hundred words.

The giraffe is one of our strangest animals. He is faster than a horse, can go longer without water than a camel, and can see behind him without turning his head.

Wind speed in the funnel of a tornado blows up to three hundred miles per hour.

A pound of peanuts contains 27.6 percent protein, but a pound of beefsteak is only 18.6 percent protein.

Grandfather clocks were invented in the late seventeenth century.

Before the use of metal razors, hairs were pulled out individually or cut by means of flints or other small stones with sharp edges.

More farmers are hurt in tractor mishaps than in any other farm-related accidents. The corn picker is the second most dangerous piece of machinery.

A primitive recipe for compounding sacred perfume is found in the Bible. See Exodus 30:34-37.

The first double-decker buses were drawn through London streets by three horses in the middle of the last century.

Apparent growth of the hair and beard after death is explained by the shrinking of the soft tissues around each individual hair.

A baby cottontail rabbit has only about one chance in nine of living long enough to become a parent.

A cup of tea contains about seventy milligrams of caffeine.

The oldest church still in use in this country is the Trinity church located in Dorchester County, Maryland. This church was built in 1675 to seat one hundred people.

Bert Loomis invented the "dribble" in basketball in 1896.

Theodore Roosevelt was the only buffalo hunter ever to become president of the United States.

Dahlias produce a sugar far superior to either cane or beet sugar.

Edward Clark, a lawyer, was the first to dream up the idea of the installment purchase plan.

There are about eighty-five thousand colonels in Kentucky.

A veterinarian of national renown advised against patting a puppy. Stroke it gently instead. Patting makes it nervous; stroking is soothing.

Of all the current major languages, Chinese is used most. More than 780 million people speak the Chinese language.

The hot fudge sundae was first dreamed up in Hollywood in 1906.

It's only three miles from the Soviet Union to the United States. That's the distance between Russia's Big Diomede Island and America's Little Diomede Island in the Bering Strait.

Nobody ever wrote a biography of Chester A. Arthur, twenty-first president of the United States.

The jack rabbit bounds between ten and fifteen feet when running fast.

A "pollyanna statement" is one to the effect that things might have been worse.

The grebe, an aquatic bird notable for its agility in water, not only eats feathers, but also feeds them to its young.

Memorial Day was observed for the first time on May 30, 1901.

More than four tons of aspirin are consumed daily in the United States.

Neither intelligence nor personality traits show up with any consistency in plain photographs.

The original *furlong* was the distance that a yoke of oxen were supposed to pull a plow without stopping to rest.

On the day a person is born, his head accounts for about one-fourth of his total body weight.

There is no definite proof that Jesus Christ could read or write Hebrew, even though He was a Jew.

The state with the highest percentage of working wives is Hawaii.

It costs about five thousand dollars to train an airline stewardess.

San Salvador is the only country in the world that inflicts the death penalty on drunken drivers—by firing squad.

17

The average person is said to swallow 295 times during the dinner hour.

One-third of all elopements end in divorce.

The typical wife prepares her husband forty meals for every meal he buys her in a restaurant.

Hard liquor sales go up about 20 percent during a recession—but it is not so with wine and beer.

In 1841, soap was so scarce and so expensive in Mexico that it was used as money.

The chance of divorce is about six times greater now than forty years ago.

In 1882, Phil Casey built the country's first handball court in Brooklyn, New York.

President Warren G. Harding coined the word *normalcy*, and President Franklin D. Roosevelt coined the word *chiseler*.

The working hours in Spain are traditionally from 10:00 A.M. to 2:00 P.M. and from 5:00 to 8:00 P.M.

The American consumption of saccharin totals several million pounds per year, with 70 percent in soft drinks.

No species of fish is known to be able to swim up a high, steep waterfall.

The *furlong*, mentioned in the Bible, was approximately twice the length of a football field.

In 1890, a New England woman used baking soda instead of cream of tartar while making peanut taffy. Her mistake become known as *peanut brittle*.

On May 31, 1790, the United States copyright law was enacted.

A "harebrained" person is one who is flighty, skittish, or reckless.

The tusks of an elephant continue to grow as long as the animal lives.

It's nine times lighter during a full moon than during a half moon.

The heart of a snake has been known to beat for twenty-four hours after its head was severed.

In self-portraits, a majority of artists tend to show more of the right side of the face than the left.

The green fat of the turtle is acclaimed for its deliciousness.

In the time of Julius Caesar, it cost about seventy-five cents to kill an enemy soldier. During the Vietnam War, it cost about $170,000.

The beaver, with nose valves that close when it goes under water, can remain submerged for as long as fifteen minutes.

William Horlick produced the first malted milk in 1882.

A tattoo needle moves up and down fifty times per second, and goes one sixty-fourth of an inch into the skin.

On the average, each family in Russia subscribes to four magazines.

Honey does not have to be digested when taken into the human body. It has already been digested in the body of the bee.

The oldest tortoise on record died at the age of 190.

It is generally agreed that Seattle, Washington, is the best restaurant town in the United States.

Mercury is the smallest planet in our solar system and is the closest to the sun.

A typical teen-ager spends approximately three hours per week on the telephone.

The human skin least sensitive to pain is that on the heel.

It takes only three pounds of feed to produce a pound of turkey, against seven pounds of feed for one pound of beef.

In Mexico avocado paste is called "poor man's butter."

The population density in the United States is fifty-eight persons per square mile.

It is estimated that 28 percent of our food intake is now in the form of snacks.

The housewife's most hated daily task is ironing.

Tokyo, Japan, is the most expensive city in the world in which to live.

Male alcoholics outnumber female alcoholics about five to one.

The average American will probably brush his teeth more than forty-five thousand times during his lifetime.

Harry Brearley, an Englishman, invented stainless steel in 1913.

It's not the peculiar rocking gait of the camel that makes the inexperienced rider sick, but the smell of the animal.

Only one state in this country is named after a president and that is the state of Washington.

No other part of the face shows age as much as the area around the eyes.

Every day in the United States, fire breaks out in more than nineteen-hundred houses and apartments.

A small, black, deep-sea fish popularly called "black swallower" sometimes swallows other fish much larger than itself.

21

In 1891, a British whaler named James Bartley was swallowed by a whale. Shortly thereafter the whale died, an operation was performed, and Mr. Bartley was rescued—still alive.

The most expensive wool is obtained from the vicuna, a camel-like animal from South Africa.

In an election year, a wife is four times as likely not to vote as her husband.

A total of forty-one Pilgrims signed the Mayflower Compact in 1620, setting up their own government and marking the beginning of democracy in America.

Statistically, the average divorced woman's first marriage lasts six years, and she then remarries at age thirty-two after waiting four years and six months.

It is possible to get a sunburn on a rainy day. Ultraviolet rays can penetrate the overcast.

The world's first cold cream was concocted by the Greek physician Galen about A.D. 150.

Baby food ranks second on the list of the most profitable food industy items.

Great Salt Lake in Utah is so salty it never freezes over entirely.

The highest gross income ever reached in a single year by a private citizen is the estimated $105 million made in 1927 by Chicago gangster Al

Capone. At the time, Capone's business card listed him as a "Second Hand Furniture Dealer."

Sex offenders are said to have a lower rate of repeat offenses than almost any type of criminal.

Lyle Goodhue invented the aerosol spray in 1941.

The average male office worker makes six trips to the washroom every working day, requiring a total of thirty minutes. The average office worker, male and female, spends two full weeks each year on coffee breaks.

There are about thirteen thousand parts in an automobile.

It takes a human being one-fifth of a second to blink his eye.

The world's best horseradish is grown near Tule Lake in northern California.

New York City was the first capital of the United States.

There are two and one-half million tons of clean air for every human being on earth.

The great W.C. Fields stored his library in his bathroom.

Studies recently conducted by a group of sociologists show that a divorced woman is an appreciably better marriage risk than a divorced man.

Spring salmon return without fail to the river of their birthplace to breed and die.

In 1830, the first fire engine was purchased for Charlotte, North Carolina, for $100.

A baseball catcher will bend his knees about three hundred times in a typical double-header.

Eskimos do not wear underwear.

A woman is most attractive between the ages of twenty-five and forty—according to an expert in such matters.

The greeting card originated in Egypt in the sixth century B.C.

At the last report, seven out of ten brides held down a job at the time of their marriage.

Americans are fitted with more than four million orthopedic casts every year.

Divorce rates have risen more than 700 percent in the last fifty years.

On August 24, 1891, Thomas A. Edison applied for a patent for a motion picture camera.

French feminine names have invaded the United States in force, with *Michelle, Renee, Nichole, Yvette,* and *Suzette* among the favorites.

It was because Handel needed money so badly that he shut himself up for twenty-one days to write the *Messiah*.

Men of science claim that people do their best thinking when the air temperature is around sixty degrees Fahrenheit.

The greatest recorded fall by a cat was 120 feet—in London, in 1965. The cat did not survive the fall.

Four musical instruments require the performer to use both hands and feet: piano, organ, harp, and drum.

Americans usually prefer the white meat of a chicken, but Frenchmen mostly go for the dark meat.

Most railroad crossing mishaps occur on Sunday.

In Nebraska it is unlawful to take or needlessly destroy the nest of any game bird.

Using pennies, nickels, dimes, quarters, and half dollars, there are exactly 293 ways to make change for a dollar.

A healthy coyote is about five miles per hour faster than a swift wolf at top speed.

The letters q, x, and z are the least used in the English language.

Norma Blancard invented the flour sifter with the crank handle in 1914.

A recent survey shows that nine out of ten remarried women think their second marriage is better than their first.

The female dog is more likely to bite than the male.

Generally, younger women get more headaches than older women.

Cookbooks outsell sex books in the United States.

One child in seven is said to be unwanted.

Stretch five thousand spider webs side by side and you'll have a ribbon one inch wide.

At the present time, two families move into Florida for every family that moves out.

Those Hollywood stunt girls who undertake daring feats in films earn around $675 per week on the average.

Statistics show that the man is more likely to commit suicide than the woman after a marriage breakup.

The brain of the dolphin is bigger than a man's.

Japan is second in the rank of the countries with the most universities, with 291.

Men reach their peak income at age fifty-six.

One out of every seven films made in Hollywood has been a western.

There are more chickens on earth than any other fowl.

In two out of three families, it's the wife who keeps the checkbook and pays the bills.

The Liberty Bell cracked on July 8, 1835, while tolling the death of Chief Justice John Marshall.

More wealthy black people live in Chicago than in any other city in America.

A psychiatrist reports that the most common word spoken by neurotic patients is *I*.

The windiest city in American isn't Chicago—it's Dodge City, Kansas.

At the time Lyndon B. Johnson was inaugurated president he was expected to live to age seventy-four. He died at sixty-four.

The average housewife runs as much risk of accident as the average baseball umpire.

The country with the largest number of citizens advertising daily in the classified sections for mates is Egypt.

A day on Jupiter is less than ten hours long because the planet rotates so swiftly.

Baby giraffes are sometimes more than six feet tall at birth.

Among athletes, the baseball players are said to be the most superstitious. Those in basketball tend to be the moodiest.

Normal, healthy persons can lose as much as one-third of their blood without fatal results.

The average-sized sugar cube is equal to one teaspoon of sugar and contains eighteen calories.

No animal or bird bleeds well if it is killed in an excited or overheated condition.

The limbs of a tree do not rise higher from the ground as the tree grows taller.

Ostriches have been known to swallow pocketbooks, spectacle cases, watches, keys, coins, stones, and iron.

The weight of the blood in the average normal adult is about one-twelfth of the body weight.

It is a well-known fact that thoroughbred horses often form a close attachment to goats. Sometimes a horse and a goat become so inseparable that the horse will become nervous and restive when the goat is taken away.

The process of stinging is generally fatal to a worker bee. When it stings deeply, the stinger is left in the victim and the bee dies.

The mound builders, a family of birds inhabiting Australia, are unique in that their young are able to fly from the moment they emerge from the shell.

Generally speaking, Old World monkeys, like man, have thirty-two teeth, while New World monkeys have thirty-six.

"Post Toasties" was originally called "Elijah's Manna."

It is not unusual for a whole family of squirrels to be albino.

The report of a gun is not as loud in dry air as it is in moist air.

Earthworms have no lungs and breathe through their skin.

The chances of hitting a jackpot in a slot machine which is not rigged in favor of the house are about one in two thousand.

The flesh of a porcupine is edible and was considered a delicacy by the Indians.

Fish don't freeze in the Arctic and Antarctic oceans because they produce their own antifreeze.

A dairy cow annually produces manure equal to about four times her body weight.

SOS has no literal meaning, but was chosen as a distress signal because of its ease in transmitting.

Opossums are prolific—the females have been known to give birth to three litters in the same year.

The speed of the average meteor is about twenty-six miles per second.

New peas float when set in a brine solution. Day-old peas sink.

Ask fifty people to quickly name any color. About thirty of them will say "Red."

The index finger is the most sensitive finger on the human hand.

A bird's foot is constructed so that it closes forcibly when the leg is bent, allowing the bird to sleep on limbs or perches.

When completed, *the new interstate highway system* will cover a total land area larger than the state of Delaware.

Nearly ten quarts of cow's milk are required to make one pound of butter.

When a person dies, all the tissues of the body do not die instantly. Some parts of the body may continue to live an hour or more after the heart stops beating.

The giraffe obtains its food chiefly by browsing on the lower branches of trees.

A watery fluid oozes from the eyes of crocodiles and alligators when they attempt to swallow something too large for them.

The Chinese first cultivated orchids over two thousand years ago.

Tens of thousands of Americans saw grapefruit for the first time at the World's Fair in Chicago in 1893.

Pound for pound, wood is stronger than steel.

Most people can hear better with their right ear than with their left.

Nuthatches are the only American birds that can walk headfirst down a tree.

Baby guinea pigs possess their second set of teeth at birth and are able to nibble on grain when only forty-eight hours old.

Horses sleep so lightly that they are awakened by the faintest sound.

The skin on a human eyelid is one-fiftieth of an inch in thickness.

Galileo first demonstrated that air has weight.

The sense of smell is more closely linked to memory than any other sense.

The average life of a worker bee during the active honey season is only about six weeks, two of which are spent in the hive.

Our word *cemetery* translated roughly out of the Latin means "dormitory for the dead."

No other American game comes close to football in the number of rules that govern play.

It often rains harder after a vivid flash of lightning and heavy peal of thunder.

Cleopatra, mistress of Julius Caesar and Mark Anthony, married two of her own brothers.

For statistical purposes some government agencies define *city* as a town with eight thousand or more inhabitants.

Sweetly scented substances that have been in Egyptian tombs for five thousand years still give off a distinct scent when the tombs are opened.

It is commonly believed that a drowning person will always rise three times before finally sinking. This belief has no scientific foundation.

Aviators have flown planes upside down for several hours to determine the physiological effects of flying in that position.

Dr. H. S. Martland was the fellow who dreamed up the term *punch-drunk,* in 1928.

About 85 billion Lincoln pennies have been minted since 1900.

The first motorcycle was a wooden machine built in 1885 in Germany, by Gottlieb Dainler—with a top speed of twelve miles per hour.

Approximately two and one-half million Americans wear a hearing aid.

An alcoholic rehabilitation center in Paterson, New Jersey, is located at the intersection of Straight and Narrow streets.

The great John Philip Sousa introduced the term *canned music* into our language.

In Japan, cremation follows death in approximately 85 percent of the cases.

An intelligent person can read at about the rate of twenty-four thousand words per hour.

Minnesota is almost the exact center of the North American continent.

Ice cream goes back hundreds of years before Christ. Its origin is credited to the Chinese who started it all by mixing fruit juice with snow.

Medical researchers insist that no animal beside man gets headaches.

If transplanted, the Great Wall of China would stretch from New York City to Omaha, Nebraska.

The letter *e* is the most useful letter of our alphabet.

On August 1, 1790, the first United States census was taken.

Among the ancient Greeks, it was not uncommon for a husband to feel his wife's pulse during their conversation if he suspected her of lying. The theory was that a person's pulse tends to pick up a few beats when the person is lying.

Light leaving the sun takes about eight minutes to reach the earth.

The first telephone directory, printed on yellow paper, was issued in 1883, in Cheyenne, Wyoming.

One of the world's rarest coins, the 1913 Liberty-head nickel, is now offered for $300,000.

It took twenty years to build the Great Pyramid in Egypt.

On August 6, 1926, talking movies were seen publicly for the first time at the Warner Theatre in New York City.

The first wife of Fyodor Vassilet, a Russian peasant, is the champion mother of all time with sixty-nine births—sixteen pairs of twins, seven sets of triplets, and four sets of quadruplets.

One cup of plain, large-kernel popcorn has twenty-five calories.

The average American working girl gets dressed each morning in sixteen minutes.

Goldfish will turn white if they are kept in a dark room.

The Kontena Indians of British Columbia require two translations of the Lord's Prayer—one masculine, one feminine.

As people with blue eyes grow older, the blue gets lighter.

There are currently more than four thousand persons in the United States who are 100 years old—or older.

The enamel on a human tooth is only one-thousandth of an inch thick.

A large dose of vitamin C and honey will neutralize a hangover—so says a famous English physician.

The person born under the sign of Leo is apt to say things with double meaning.

At age eighty a Colorado man discovered that he had spent five years of his life waiting on people, three months scolding children, six months tying neckties, and eight days telling dogs to lie down and be quiet.

The Apaches were the first Indians to own horses.

Jesus Christ lived on this earth for about twelve thousand days before He was crucified.

Old-school Japanese mothers never kiss their babies.

In total darkness, the healthy human eye has the extraordinary capacity to see the light of a single candle up to fourteen miles away.

Some twins have been born as much as seven days apart.

Among domesticated animals, the swine is the greatest carrier of disease.

The moose does a lot of grazing on its knees because of its short neck.

One out of every twenty American teen-agers owns his own TV set.

March is said to be the month in which children sleep most soundly.

In a race between a grayhound and a coyote, you'd better count on the coyote.

A fishhook doesn't hurt the fish since a fish can feel practically no pain.

Numerous experts claim that a bachelor is a better credit risk than a single working woman.

Pecans were discovered in Louisiana in 1541.

The stomach of a hippopotamus is more than ten feet long and can hold more than four hundred pounds of food.

About 60 percent of California's population lives in the eight southernmost counties.

When something is as "smooth as glass," it's 300 times smoother than satin and 475 times smoother than silk.

Michigan was the first state to abolish the death penalty—in 1847.

A human being couldn't fly even if he had wings—the breastbone isn't strong enough.

A two-ounce serving of cooked beef liver provides more than thirty thousand international units of vitamin A.

The longest reign as a world champion is the twenty-seven years of tennis player Pierre Etchbaster, who retired at the age of sixty.

Americans consume more than 750 million gallons of ice cream every year.

The five most boring jobs in the world are: assembly line worker, pool typist, bank guard, elevator operator, and housewife.

On April 10, 1865, President Abraham Lincoln made his last public speech.

The heart of a healthy grownup pumps six and one-half tons of blood per day.

On April 10, 1969, the first human recipient of an artificial heart died in Houston, Texas, after living sixty-three hours with the new heart.

Statistics show that Americans suffer between 230 and 500 million colds each year.

Jumbo, a circus attraction for P. T. Barnum, was reported to be the largest elephant in the world with a height of twelve feet and a weight of seven tons.

There is another Indian village in South Dakota near Wounded Knee. It's named "Sprained Ankle."

Water is 773 times heavier than air.

The ear of a fish is internal, imbedded in the skull, and is used as a balancing organ to detect vibrations.

There are seventy breweries in the United States.

The closest thing to a perfect counterfeit note was an 1891 one hundred dollar bill. It was so close to being perfect that the Secretary of the Treasury recalled all such currency that year.

An Emory University scientist estimates that a person between the ages of thirty and eighty loses an average of ten thousand brain cells per day.

On April 7, 1891, Nebraska took a radical step and introduced the first eight-hour work day.

Lawmen tell us that 48 percent of rape victims are acquainted with their assailants.

Robert ranks number 3 on the list of popular names for boys.

Potato chips and doughnuts were invented by accident.

Abraham Lincoln could split six hundred rails in twelve hours.

The United States has 3,800,000 miles of roads and streets.

The antelope is the fastest of all North American animals.

Towels and washcloths last only an average of five years; sheets and pillowcases last an average of seven years.

The modern American woman spends 75 percent of her time sitting down.

When Caesar and Cleopatra were romancing, he was fifty-four and she was twenty-one.

The squirrel uses his tail as a parachute and for balancing.

On April 15, 1923, insulin became available for general use.

The ant colony, like the beehive, is always run by one queen.

In 75 percent of matrimonial engagements now, the woman is said to court the man.

Ottmar Mergenthaler invented the linotype in 1884.

The Greek philosopher Thales accurately predicted an eclipse of the sun in 585 B.C.

A powerful laser beam can melt a glass rod so that it can be reduced to hair-thin fiber almost a mile long.

As of 1974, two hours and thirty-eight minutes of the average American's eight-hour working day went toward paying his taxes.

There are fifty-four mountains in the United States taller than Pikes Peak.

A rattlesnake two minutes old can coil and strike expertly.

Sixteen states have made snoring by either a husband or a wife a legitimate ground for divorce.

The North Pole gets 120 more hours of sunlight over the course of a year than the South Pole.

Young ladies' hair grows fastest in their late teens.

A recent survey shows that 12 percent of all Americans would settle in some other country if they could afford it.

The big robber crab of the South Pacific likes to climb palm trees, usually in an attempt to steal coconuts.

A dragonfly can use its feet for perching on a limb, but its legs are useless for walking.

In a 1910 experiment, a flea jumped thirteen inches and got as high as seven and one-half inches off the ground.

The female ant will lay as many as one hundred thousand eggs about every five weeks.

In 1779 the British Parliament gave serious consideration to a bill that called for punishing women who used perfumes and cosmetics to lure men into matrimony. The bill would have made such marriages illegal.

Fifty-one percent of the American people believe that unidentified flying objects are from outer space.

It's believed that there's no country in the world where children do not play "hide-and-seek."

The ancient Romans thought it unwise to enter a house with the left foot first.

A team of medical experts in Virginia contends that you're more likely to catch the common cold viruses by shaking hands than by kissing.

Cancer is the leading cause of death in school children in the United States.

More tea is grown on the north side of the equator than on the south.

Farm ponds properly designed and built can produce from one hundred to three hundred pounds of catfish per acre each year.

It was Abraham Lincoln who said that the ballot is stronger than the bullet.

The first president to live in the White House was John Adams.

After age twenty, the older you get the less sleep you need, until age sixty.

White paint is black before the can or bucket is opened.

West German children go to school six days a week until age eighteen.

Seven out of ten wars during the last 155 years have been won by the people who started them.

A bullet gets cooler after it leaves the rifle muzzle.

You can't lose weight by perspiring profusely despite what many people believe.

The middle of a watermelon isn't red until it's cut.

A female carp may produce more than two million eggs each year.

The giraffe has no vocal chords.

Cancer researchers at a Glasgow hospital have taught chickens how to smoke cigarettes. They soon get hooked—the hens become irritable if they don't get at least one-half cigarette every other day.

The average fifty-year-old man needs only seven hours and fifteen minutes sleep per night.

When gloves were first invented, they had no fingers. The Romans introduced gloves with fingers.

The steel guitar was invented by a Hawaiian instrumentalist by the name of Joseph Kekuku about 1895.

On April 21, 1856, the first railroad bridge across the Mississippi River was completed.

Chili con carne and hot tamales are not Mexican dishes. Both were created in southern Texas.

Some medical authorities contend emotions, not the heat of the day, account for most perspiration.

The first mail carriers in this country worked on commission only. They pocketed ten cents for each letter and one cent for each newspaper they delivered.

United States senators were originally elected by the state legislature. Not until 1913 was an amendment passed calling for their direct election.

On April 27, 1937, the first United States social security payment was made.

The heaviest wood is black ironwood, which weighs 9.3 pounds per cubic foot.

Eggs of the gar fish are poisonous and should never be eaten.

The Pentagon was completed in 1943 at a cost of $83 million.

Among retired couples, women drivers considerably outnumber men drivers.

The British eat more candy per capita than any other people in the world.

Your heart spends more time at rest than working. If you live to be seventy years old, your heart will have been at rest for about forty years.

It costs twice as much money to ship a corpse on a train as the price of a first-class ticket for a living human being.

On April 22, 1954, Congress ordered that "In God We Trust" be stamped on all coins.

The lowest point in North America is at Badwater, in California's Death Valley.

Concerning office dictionaries—one out of eight nationwide is more than twenty years old.

The water is so clear in the Valdez Peninsula in Argentina that it is possible to see to a depth of one hundred feet.

About seventy-five thousand horses are slaughtered every year in the United States for food.

Harry S. Truman was the first president of the United States to ride in a submarine.

It was the custom in Rome to pay soldiers partly with salt formed into the shape of coins and called *salarium.* This is the Latin word from which the English word *salary* is derived.

Basketball is played in 190 countries.

The first wrapped candy bar appeared in American baseball parks in 1911.

There are more hunting and fishing licenses issued in California than in any other state.

President Woodrow Wilson's wife, Edith, was a descendant of the Indian princess Pocahontas.

On April 25, 1901, New York became the first state to require automobile licenses.

The only species of catfish with a forked tail are the channel cat and the blue cat.

Trinity, a dachshund owned by a Minnesota bride, carried rings tied to a white satin dumbbell at her mistress' wedding.

The world's largest bay is the Bay of Bengal, with a shoreline of 2,250 miles.

Porpoises can stay under water for about five minutes without breathing.

The average American eats more than seven pounds of pickles per year.

A cupful of gasoline packs the energy of five sticks of dynamite.

Young wives seldom buy cottage cheese or laxatives.

Hawaii is the only state in the Union with but one school district.

Fifty-four percent of American farm families don't keep dogs.

We get a month without a full moon about five times every one hundred years—always during February.

On April 7, 1927, the first successful demonstration of long distance television was made between Washington and New York City.

Solomon and Aristotle were both extremely fond of honey.

Using a mechanical tree-planting machine, a two-man crew can plant as many as ten thousand trees in one day.

At least one-fifth of the average grocery store bill goes for nonfood items such as pantyhose, detergents, mouth wash, and paper plates.

American parents talk with their youngsters only about twenty minutes a week on the average, according to a University of Wisconsin researcher.

In 1975, Baskin Tipps of Cincinnati, Ohio, learned to read and write at the age of eighty-four.

The oreosome fish has no scales—only horns.

In Finland, far more boy babies than girl babies are conceived during the first month of marriage.

Twelve percent of American children develop a goiter.

Enrico Caruso was the first singer to leave his voice to posterity by way of the phonograph.

The "Rocky Mountain," or "bighorn," sheep do not have coats of wool.

Thomas Jefferson wrote the Declaration of Independence in eighteen days.

The average American can now expect to live 71.4 years.

Bill Picket, a black cowboy, is credited with originating the rodeo art of bulldogging.

Only about one-third of the homes in East and West Germany have a bathroom.

Numerous black bears starve to death—because the quills of a porcupine have become stuck in their tongue.

At age four, the average child will speak as many as twelve thousand words per day.

A doctor of renown contends that the woman who describes her husband as "the most wonderful man in the world" probably needs psychiatric treatment.

Cats can suffer from sunburn, especially white cats which have no skin pigment to protect them.

Brushing your tongue as well as your teeth three times a day will reduce up to 90 percent of decay-causing bacteria in the mouth.

White blackberries were developed by Luther Burbank.

When Albert Einstein was a college professor, he never wore socks to his classes.

The tail of the beaver is used to help the animal stand erect.

Up to and including 1965, France and England had each fought nineteen wars.

The sperm whale can stay submerged for an hour or more.

On May 6, 1851, a patent for the manufacture of ice was granted to Dr. John Gorrie of Florida.

The American toad may lay as many as fifteen thousand eggs, but less than one tadpole in one hundred will live to maturity.

Bananas breathe. They inhale oxygen, exhale carbon dioxide, and generate their own heat.

A moth has no mouth or stomach.

No other fruit matures so slowly as the seed coconut which takes about ten years to ripen.

In the wild, dogs run in a pack and follow a leader—but cats don't.

Mary Anderson invented the windshield wiper in 1902.

On May 10, 1872, Victoria Woodhull was nominated as the first woman for president.

Sugar wasn't added to coffee until this beverage became popular in western Europe in the seventeenth century.

Abraham Lincoln was paid $55.70 annually as postmaster of New Salem, Indiana.

Only one out of every fourteen women in the United States has blond hair, and only one out of every sixteen men.

The world's largest rodent, the capybara, measures four feet from head to tail.

California has more native lilies than any other state.

Very few spiders live more than two years.

Salem is the most common name for a town in the United States—with twenty-four towns so named.

People swallow about eight times per hour when they're asleep.

The athletic budgets in the average high school will run about ninety-nine dollars per boy and one dollar per girl.

Approximately thirty-five thousand women in France pay income tax on money gained from prostitution.

Washington, D.C. has the highest rate of cirrhosis per capita in the United States.

Swiss watchmakers use a little machine so fine that it can split a human hair lengthwise into fifty equal strands.

In New England there's a "Sit, Whittle, and Spit" men's club. The charter only sets down three rules: 1. Don't sit in the sun. 2. Don't whittle toward yourself. 3. Don't spit against the wind.

A recent survey shows that husbands don't tend to be as critical of their wives as do wives of their husbands.

On May 9, 1754, the first newspaper cartoon appeared in Franklin's "Join or Die."

Narcotic addiction is forty times greater among doctors than among other professionals.

The average driver gets a ticket every 9.2 years for running a red light, speeding, or reckless driving.

Living with in-laws is always a little risky, but recent studies indicate it's less risky to live with the husband's parents than with the wife's.

A Georgia man, Joseph H. McKellar, is the national champion watermelon-seed spitter. In 1975, he propelled a watermelon seed thirty-six feet, two and one-half inches from a stationary position.

The largest nuts ever made weigh 2,912 pounds each. They are used for securing the propellers of a ship.

Radium is three thousand times more valuable than gold.

The average longevity for a guinea pig, mouse, and opossum is the same—four years.

Life expectancy of a car on the road nowadays is exactly ten years and three months.

The greatest number of lynchings in the United States in the twentieth century occurred in 1901—with 130 instances.

It takes about two weeks for those nicotine stains on your fingers to go away after you quit smoking.

Statisticians report that the average American doctor drives sixty-two miles per day.

Snakes sleep with their eyes open because they have no eyelids.

President Harry S. Truman authorized production of the hydrogen bomb on January 31, 1950.

An oyster can make an average-size pearl in about five years.

There are twenty-seven bones in the wrist, palm, and five fingers.

About two out of every five men admitted to state mental hospitals are alcoholics.

The tiny kangaroo rat that lives in the desert exists without ever drinking.

On May 16, 1866, the first nickels were authorized by the United States Treasury Department.

The world's largest zipper is in the Houston Astrodome. It zips the turf together.

Experts recently found that saliva increases measurably during the telling of a lie.

The year following 1 B.C. was A.D. 1.

Clockmakers sell new grandfather clocks as fast as they produce them.

John Tyler was the first vice president to become president of the United States.

A second marriage is about 50 percent riskier than a first marriage—according to an analysis of census figures.

The game of contract bridge was invented by Harold Vanderbilt in 1921.

More cowboys have drowned in fording swollen rivers than those who have died in gun fights.

One-fourth of all car crackups are rear-end collisions.

On August 10, 1833, Chicago was incorporated as a village of about two hundred people.

New Orleans is five feet below sea level, making it the lowest point in Louisiana.

Michigan was the first state to develop roadside parks and picnic tables.

Goats are odorless except during the mating season.

In thirty-seven years the world population will double its size if the present 2 percent annual rate of growth continues.

The average shower bath consumes twenty to

thirty gallons of water while a tub bath uses thirty to forty gallons.

If you're caught without a ruler for a simple measuring job, it helps to know that a dollar bill is exactly six and one-eighth inches long.

The shortest navigable crossing of the Pacific Ocean is 10,905 miles long.

It takes only 8.3 minutes for light to travel from the sun to earth and 1.28 seconds from the moon to earth.

The tallest recorded bamboo tree stood 115 feet tall—in Burma, in 1904.

A person who collects picture postcards is a *deltiologist*.

An oyster reaches maturity in three years.

A professor of science says that all birds flirt.

Lucy is now among the preferred names for newborn girls in Africa.

By general agreement, if a man is over six feet, seven inches tall, he's regarded as a giant.

American Indians taught the early settlers how to make maple syrup.

One fathom of water is six feet deep.

The ancient Greeks and Romans never knew anything about sugar.

On April 27, 1970, Peter Morrow of Brisbane, Australia, ate seven pounds and three ounces of ice cream in thirty minutes.

The eggs of the rainbow snake more than double in size after being laid.

Based on the average life expectancy, when you were twenty years old, you have 21,900 tomorrows ahead of you.

Wood burns best when it is one to two years old.

In 1883, Mississippi College in Clinton, Mississippi, became the first co-educational college in the United States to grant degrees to women.

The cormorant, which has no nostrils, breathes through its mouth.

Milk was delivered to customers in bottles for the first time in 1878.

If the strength of a two-hundred-pound man was in proportion to that of an earthworm, he would be able to move six tons.

Just as gloves have a place for each finger today, so the socks in ancient Rome had a place for each toe.

Pretzels have been in existence since A.D. 610.

On May 20, 1883, the first railroad table was published by the Baltimore and Ohio Railroad.

In Chicago, a woman driver can be ticketed if either her hair or hat covers one eye.

George Washington refused to shake hands with anybody during his two terms as president of the United States. He bowed instead.

A jogger who burns up one hundred calories during his daily run could lose ten pounds per year.

The first policeman to use a whistle to direct traffic was Captain Barnard Hoppe of the Boston police force in 1908.

In daylight, deer are the most intelligent and elusive of all wild animals.

The average American man spends four hours each year tying his necktie.

In New York City, about three hundred people per year have tight-fitting rings removed from their fingers.

The first cookbook was written by Platina, librarian to the Vatican in Rome, and was published in 1474.

Every cubic foot of garbage can be a breeding ground for seventy-five thousand flies.

Monday is the day of the week when hospital emergency rooms get the most business.

One pound of processed and enriched uranium

can produce enough electricity to light a 100-watt bulb for twenty-six hundred years.

The Goodyear Tire and Rubber Company has manufactured the world's largest tire—a twelve-footer, weighing seven thousand pounds.

Digitalis was first introduced into scientific medicine in 1785, by William Withering, an Englishman.

A California firm specializes in insuring the life and health of cats and dogs.

The word *hippopotamus* means "river horse," indicating the area in which this animal lives.

"Dreft" was the first of the household detergents.

Only 3 percent of the American people read one book each year.

On May 28, 1863, the first Negro regiment left Boston for the front during the Civil War.

The tallest married couple in the world was Mr. and Mrs. Martin Bates. She was seven feet, five and one-half inches tall and her husband was a few inches shorter. They were married on June 17, 1871.

The driver most apt to lose control of a car when a tire blows out on a freeway is the girl under twenty.

The bison always faces into a storm.

One-eighth of the adult population of Louisiana has less than a fifth-grade education.

St. Augustine, Florida, in existence since 1565, is the oldest continually inhabited city in the United States.

Aristotle, the Greek philosopher, was a stutterer.

The paradise fish must surface for air or it will drown.

North Dakota is the only state in the Union never to have recorded an earthquake.

Roses that are cut in the afternoon last considerably longer than those cut in the morning.

Flora May Jackson, known as "Baby Flo," was five feet tall and weighed 840 pounds.

Statistics show that couples who get married in January, February, and March wind up with the highest divorce rate. June marriages produce the lowest rate.

Oklahoma's state capital is the only capital building in the world that has a producing oil well under it.

It is a matter of record that the great Seneca complained mightily during the year A.D. 61 about air pollution in Rome.

The largest ice cream sundae ever made was constructed by Bob Bercaw of Wooster, Ohio, in

1971. He used forty-two flavors of ice cream covered by fifty pounds of chocolate fudge.

One person in every nine thousand in the United States is an albino.

An old California law makes a housewife liable to imprisonment if she doesn't boil her dustcloth.

Dentists contend that forty-nine out of every fifty citizens have at least one crooked tooth.

Eli Bowen, of Richland County, Ohio, was born in 1844 without legs. Two feet of different size grew directly out of his hip joints.

At least half of the Eskimos in the world have never seen an igloo.

A solar eclipse occurs in some part of the world about every eighteen months.

The first automobile show in the United States was held in New York's Madison Square Garden in 1900.

Almost one out of four women doctors is a pediatrician.

A horse is measured by "hands." A hand is equal to four inches.

There are about half as many Christmas cards sold every year as there are people on earth.

Benjamin Franklin is said to have preferred the turkey instead of the eagle as our national emblem.

There is no evidence that the killer whale ever killed anybody.

Many men, but few women, have been impostors.

Pennsylvania Hospital, the first hospital in the United States, was founded on May 11, 1751.

At age twenty-two, Robert Wardlow was 8 feet, 11.1 inches tall. He was born in Alton, Illinois, on February 22, 1918.

About one-half million cataract operations are performed every year in the United States.

The first mechanical lawn mower was invented by an Englishman named Edwin Budding, in 1831.

Austria has the highest rate of accidental death of any country in the world.

About one-third of New Mexico's residents are of Mexican-American heritage.

The United States president who stayed closest to the White House during his term of office was Abraham Lincoln.

Dipel, a natural bacterium product, kills caterpillars but is harmless to other living things.

A worried, depressed, and negative attitude can give you flat feet—so says a doctor at the Southern California Medical School.

The first rules of usage for the American flag weren't adopted until 1923—146 years after Betsy Ross sewed the Stars and Stripes.

Soap has been made from silk worms by Pakistanis.

The slimy substance produced by a fish's skin helps prevent bacteria and disease.

A robust belly laugh injects six times as much oxygen into the system as a deep breath.

The first American amusement park, Lake Compounce, opened in Bristol, Connecticut, more than one hundred years ago.

Insect sting kills more people in the United States each year than snakebite, according to the American Medical Association.

Girls who work as file clerks wear out more sheer stockings than girls in any other job.

People who don't know much about music tend to hear it better in the left ear than in the right.

The world has been at peace during only 8 percent of the last thirty-five hundred years of recorded history.

Babies born in the summer months are less likely to develop mental ailments as they grow up.

The spitting cobra can blind a threatening animal with a spray of venom at a distance of about eight feet.

Each year termites strike five times as many homes as fire.

President Theodore Roosevelt lost his mother and his wife on the same day—February 14, 1884.

In 1974, Milt Harper of San Francisco wore a mustache that measured twenty-four inches tip to tip.

American feet have been growing almost one full size every generation. Today the average American male wears size ten.

On June 8, 1872, penny postcards were first authorized by the United States Congress.

On the average, the calves of girls' legs today are slightly larger than thirty-five years ago.

Chicago and St. Louis get 15 percent more rain than do the towns around them. Heat rising from the buildings is the reason.

The ancient Greeks made napkins out of asbestos and never washed them. They just placed them in the fire after the meal to burn them clean.

Medical men say that tall women don't seem to suffer as much during childbirth as short women.

The rainbow trout gets its name from the red stripe often plainly visible along its sides.

A cobra can kill an elephant if it bites the tip of its trunk or the base of its toenail.

The American pulp and paper industry uses more than 4 trillion gallons of water each year.

Vivian "Sailor Joe" Simmons, a Canadian tattoo artist, had 4,831 tattoos on his body.

When a duck dives under water, its heartbeat immediately slows to less than one-half the normal rate.

The garden pest known as the *slug* is known to be very fond of beer.

Las Vegas, Nevada, has more churches per capita than any other town in the world.

The Parent-Teachers Association (PTA) was organized at Crystal Springs, Maryland, in October, 1909.

It takes six live geese to produce one pound of the best pillow feathers.

The first American cookbook was published in 1796.

Robert L. Foster of California held his breath for thirteen minutes, forty-two and one-half seconds in a swimming pool.

The merry-go-round is the most popular ride at amusement parks.

Statistics show that a hunter is sixty-seven times more likely to be killed in a car accident on the way to the hunt than when actually hunting.

The greatest number of bee stings survived by a human is 2,443, by Johanne Relleke in Rhodesia, on January 28, 1962.

In Japan most of the golf caddies are women.

Mongolians rarely become bald. The same is true of American Indians.

The first Negro senator in the United States was Hiram R. Revels of Mississippi, who was elected in 1870.

In Norway the housewife is guaranteed by law a week-long annual vacation.

Hyperacusia is an odd ailment of the human ear. The victims develop an acute sense of hearing. Doctors report that one victim was able to hear the ticking of a watch thirty feet away.

In 1719 the first street lantern in this country was erected in Boston.

The first sulfa drug was used in therapy by Dr. Gerhard Domgak, a German physician, in 1932.

The first Ku Klux Klan was started on Christmas Eve in 1865 by six young Confederate veterans at Pulaski, Tennessee.

Records show that three out of every five men who go into the life insurance business quit within twelve months.

The difference between a great race horse and a good race horse is only a few seconds.

A freshman pre-engineering student at Moorhead State College in Moorhead, Minnesota, built a bridge of toothpicks capable of holding 816 pounds.

The elephant, if properly taught, can throw a baseball faster than a baseball pitcher.

Americans are spending $570 million per year on donuts made with and without the hole.

The record high temperature in the United States is 134 degrees, recorded on July 10, 1913, in Death Valley, California.

Alabama ships more queen bees worldwide than any other state.

The whale has seven cervical vertebrae.

Motel managers say a traveling man rarely complains of the service if he is alone. This is not so if he is accompanied by his wife.

The world's oldest existing piano was put together by one Bartolomen Christofori in Florence, Italy, in 1720.

Just about all the great screen lovers have been dark haired.

Loss of vitamin A and C occurs when vegetable tissues are bruised.

Charles W. Pearle was America's first taxidermist.

The pledge of allegiance to the flag was first published in the September, 1892, issue of *Youth's Companion*, a weekly magazine.

In the next twelve months the people of the United States will consume somewhere around twenty thousand tons of aspirin.

It's a matter of historical record that President Teddy Roosevelt kept a .44 caliber Smith and Wesson revolver at arm's length from his pillow in the White House.

The Siberian tiger is the largest and fiercest cat. Males can weigh more than five hundred pounds, stand five feet tall at the shoulder, and stretch fourteen feet.

Before Henry Ford set up his assembly line, it took the automakers twelve hours and thirty minutes to put a car together.

The wealthiest 5 percent of the American population owns 83 percent of all corporate stocks.

Snow falls at the rate of about two and one-half miles per hour.

The average peach tree dies in eight years.

No flower blooms longer than the orchid.

Giraffes communicate with one another mainly by switching their tail.

The annual southward migration of the grey

whale to breeding grounds off Baja, California, begins the first week in December.

McCurtain County, Oklahoma, is the holly capital of the United States, and is the home of the nation's largest field of holly.

Accidents in which children are hit by a car occur most frequently in the month of May.

Government statistics reveal that depressive illnesses account for 23.3 percent of admissions to mental hospitals.

The heart of a giraffe weighs up to twenty pounds more than the human heart.

There are four color classes of honey: white, golden, amber, and dark.

You can depreciate a $25,000 elephant about $1,666 every year.

Spiders have been seen floating on strands of silk as high as two and one-half miles above the earth.

The gorilla is the largest ape in the world.

Angel Falls, In Venezuela, is the highest waterfall in the world with a drop of 3,212 feet.

George Thiess of Dallas, Texas, is the inventor of the electronic digital wrist watch—in 1968.

William Shakespeare had three brothers: Gilbert, Richard, and Edmund.

A thirsty camel could easily drink a whole bathtub full of water without stopping.

The nightmares of women tend to be more terrifying than those of men.

Widows of Asmat tribesmen in New Guinea roll in mud to mourn their husband.

A canary's pulse beats approximately one thousand times per minute.

A newborn whale is almost as long as its mother and half as heavy.

The cotton gin was first put to use in Washington, Georgia, in 1783.

Fiddler on the Roof holds the record for the most Broadway performances: 3,242.

A sugar mill is one of the buildings on the campus of Louisiana State University in Baton Rouge.

There are more than two hundred miles of scenic road in Yosemite National Park.

Bighorn sheep can lie in the snow for hours and stay warm because their winter coat of matted hair allows so little body heat to escape—not even enough to melt a snowflake!

Alfalfa is the world's oldest and most important forage crop.

The world's last thoroughbred Angora cat was reported in Turkey in 1907.

In the United States there are at least twenty-five thousand suicides recorded annually.

The sixty-member Lowell High School Band of San Francisco played thirty-one hours of continuous music, ending Sunday afternoon, March 16, 1975.

More than two hundred and fifty years ago in Boston a teacher's salary was approximately thirty-five cents per week—so we're told.

In the animal world, only monkeys and apes see color.

On June 29, 1969, the first worship service to be led by a Jewish rabbi was conducted in the White House.

If all widowers in the United States lived together, their colony would be the fifth largest American city.

The table fork was first introduced in America by John Winthrop, on June 25, 1630.

A certain "Jim Marshall" gets credit for starting the famous California Gold Rush in 1848.

It is impossible to light a match on the moon.

Half the car wrecks in the United States occur at speeds of forty miles per hour or less.

A purse snatcher in Haiti is subject to the death penalty.

In China a person is not accepted as a mature adult until he is forty. Before that time, he is not permitted to speak his mind in the presence of the wise.

At one time or another, rice has served as money in many nations.

The first Mother's Day service was held in Andrews Methodist Church in Grafton, West Virginia, on May 10, 1908.

Americans write more than 23 billion checks each year.

Certain species of bamboo grow thirty-six inches per day.

The Gulf of Mexico has a shoreline thirty-one hundred miles long.

New Hampshire is the only state that permits a girl to marry at age thirteen—with parental consent.

The elephant is, or can be, the most dangerous animal in the world.

A book on automotive repair is the one most likely to be stolen from a public library.

Chewing gum was first manufactured in this country in 1848 at Bangor, Maine, by John Curtis and his brother.

Sixty percent of the working population in metropolitan Los Angeles drives to work.

New Mexico has two state vegetables—the pinto bean and the chili bean.

In 1851, Maine became the first state to enact a prohibition law.

The Brazilian anteater's tongue is eighteen inches long.

Ray Schmit of St. Cloud, Minnesota, owns thirty-two Edsels—the car produced by the Ford Motor Company between 1958 and 1960.

Look at your watch! In less than two minutes one person in the United States will die of cancer.

There are more blondes in California than in any other state.

The expression "It's raining cats and dogs" is said to have originated in England in the seventeenth century.

Polar bears have been sighted eighty miles out at sea. They swim this distance although they use only their front legs when swimming; their hind legs remain motionless.

On July 2, 1862, the Congress of the United States ordered all federal officeholders to swear an oath of loyalty to the government.

The diamond—hardest material known to man—cuts, drills, grinds, and polishes better than anything else.

Blue, black and green ink are used in printing a United States dollar bill.

Goslings accept as their mother the first living thing they see.

The average person in the United States receives eight pieces of mail each week.

Our children are 10 percent taller and fifteen to thirty pounds heavier than the children of a century ago.

Under ultraviolet light, a white man's tooth ground to powder glows green, a black man's tooth glows a reddish orange.

People who earn the lowest wages eat the most vitamins.

Among the various guns used by sportsmen throughout the world, the shotgun is the most popular.

In Massachusetts the women outnumber the men 100 to 93.

We are now told that the highest rate of divorce and suicide is among dentists.

Thomas A. Edison announced his invention of the phonograph on November 21, 1877.

One cow in thirty thousand gives birth to triplets.

A gold snuffbox once owned by Queen Frederika, the former queen mother of Greece, was sold in London for $206,400.

Insomnia affects about two million people in the United States.

William Howard Taft weighed 350 pounds when he was president of the United States.

Hal Davis of Santa Ana, California, has collected thirteen hundred nutcrackers over the past twenty years.

For every woman college professor, there are four men.

Despite his financial holdings, George Washington had to borrow money to buy a new suit for his inauguration as president of the United States.

The tongue of the blue whale weighs more than an average-size elephant.

About 87 percent of husbands and wives in the United States sleep in the same bed—each will shift their sleeping position approximately thirty-five times per night.

A mail boat delivers mail six days a week to residents living along the bayous of coastal Louisiana.

Research reveals that most hard-core pornography is sold to middle-class men over thirty-five.

Worldwide there are only 5.6 telephones to every 100 people.

The first steamer to cross the Atlantic Ocean was the *Yorkshire* which sailed from Liverpool to New York in November, 1846.

One hundred years ago in Boston, bananas sold for one dollar each.

Americans buy enough automobile tires in an average year to circle the earth more than four times.

One in every ten shoppers in the supermarket winds up at the checkout counter without enough money to pay the tab.

An ant can pull ten times its own weight.

Old paper money is no longer burned by the United States government. To avoid pollution it is pulverized.

The highest known mountain in the world is Mount Everest, with a height of 20,002 feet.

In 1974, twelve thousand Americans needed a kidney transplant.

A medium-size plum contains only twenty-five calories.

It's the female horsefly, not the male, who bites the horse.

The people of the United States use the most

chewing gum of any nation in the world. In 1974, Americans spent more than $670 million for chewing gum.

Women who like math tend to be good drivers. Women who like literature tend to be good cooks.

The albatross is a marine bird with a wing span up to seven feet.

Legend says that the first Roquefort cheese was accidentally discovered on June 4, 1070.

Statistics reveal that only 7 percent of the people of the United States think for themselves.

About one out of four appointments keep you waiting.

It's not unusual for a dolphin to grow five pounds per month in its first two years.

The first train in the United States drawn by steam made a run from Albany to Schenectady, New York, on August 9, 1831.

Arrows used for hunting deer and antelope in Nebraska must have a total cutting edge of at least three inches.

The comic strip "Little Orphan Annie" was created in 1924.

Two out of three children in New Zealand smoke cigarettes before they are seven years old.

The driest place on earth may be the Atacama Desert in Chile, where no measurable rainfall has been recorded for many years.

Most American citizens prefer the sales tax over any other sort of tax.

One half of a medium-size cantaloupe contains about sixty calories, and enough vitamin A and C to supply more than the recommended daily amount for adults.

The tail of the beaver has been considered a delicacy since the first settlement in America.

Watermarks on writing paper were first made in Italy in the thirteenth century.

Queen Berengaria, wife of Richard the Lionhearted, was never in England.

The most healthy place to live is where the average temperature varies at least three degrees from day to day in the summer and seven degrees in the winter.

Food packed in green containers sells best.

John Quincy Adams and Dwight D. Eisenhower possessed one physical characteristic not possessed by other presidents—baldness.

A jockey's riding clothes, including his boots, seldom weighs more than thirty ounces.

The late Rudolph Valentino, a romantic movie

star, introduced the tango in the United States in 1914.

Only purebred Jersey cows are permitted on the channel island of Jersey.

One hundred pounds of potatoes will produce about twenty-five pounds of potato chips.

The powerful grizzly bear has been timed running up to thirty miles per hour.

Only one out of every twenty-five rattlesnakes rattles before he strikes.

Contrary to popular belief, the legs of a newborn colt are not full length at birth.

More than 50 out of every 100 Americans wear glasses.

The fastest escalator in the world—at Leicester Square subway station in London—travels at a speed of 180 feet per minute.

Primo Carnera of Italy was the heaviest world champion in boxing, weighing 265 pounds.

On July 13, 1863, riots protesting the draft broke out in New York City during the Civil War.

Experts estimate there are 10 million compulsive gamblers in the United States. One out of every four gamblers is a woman.

The golden eagle may stand three feet high,

weigh around ten pounds, have a seven-foot wing spread, and live to be thirty years old.

Only a few spiders, including the black widow, can bite hard enough to penetrate human skin.

The mallard is considered to be the most popular duck.

Customarily, when Mexicans wave good-bye to you, they motion toward themselves, not you.

The first adding machine was invented in 1642 by a Frenchman named Pascal.

Maple syrup is produced only in the United States and Canada.

The average American husband is six inches taller than his wife.

None of our presidents was as poor a speller as Harry S. Truman.

The poisonous snake that bites the most people in the United States is the copperhead.

One in every four Americans won't eat liver, no matter how it's fixed.

The world record for continuous telephone conversation has been established by students at Morehead State College in Morehead, Kentucky. The conversation lasted 724 hours.

Medical records indicate that about four thousand Americans have lost the physical sense of smell.

It is said that a man is far more likely to remember his first paycheck than his first kiss.

On July 29, 1914, the first transcontinental telephone line opened for business.

In the United States, there is only one doctor for every twenty-four hundred rural folk compared to one doctor for every five hundred city dwellers.

The practice of polygamy was officially abandoned by the Mormon church in 1890.

At least ten thousand Americans are bitten each year by a dog.

In 1861, Congress abolished flogging in the United States Army.

Many people believe that monkeys cannot swim without being taught. This is a mistaken idea.

Fifty-six-year-old Victor Solow of Mamaroneck, New York, was dead for twenty-three minutes after suffering a heart attack. Electric shocks brought him back to life.

The common toad sheds its outer skin several times a year.

In Thailand there are an uneven number of steps in every staircase.

During the Second World War, noisy or squeaky shoes became fashionable in England.

Adult sea otters, weighing 45 to 100 pounds, eat the equivalent of one-fifth or more of their weight in food every day.

At full speed a thoroughbred horse can go as fast as forty miles per hour carrying 125 pounds or more on his back.

Because the eyes of the owl are immovable, it must swivel its head to shift its line of sight.

A person who carries the left hind foot of a rabbit in his pocket, particularly a rabbit that has run in a graveyard, is said to be assured of good luck.

"Lassie" first appeared on TV in 1954.

Raccoons in captivity have been known to live more than ten years.

It is proper to mend a United States flag when torn unless it is in such bad condition that it would be a discredit to the owner if displayed.

Samuel Clemens signed his name as "Mark Twain" for the first time on February 2, 1863.

A typical heavy London fog contains 820,000 dust particles to the cubic inch.

The present size of the baseball bat was adopted about 1860.

Although beavers are aquatic in habit and spend a great deal of time in the water, they never touch fish or any other animal food.

The common housefly does not breed in Alaska.

In Europe the stork is regarded with a feeling bordering on reverence.

An estimated two out of three Americans do not smoke.

A chimney swallow can fly at a speed of 100 miles per hour.

The human brain attains almost its full, adult size during the first six years of a child's life.

Modern greyhounds can run more than sixty miles per hour and some of them can bound eighteen feet in a single stride.

It is not uncommon for young fathers to suffer from morning sickness or strange cravings for certain foods similar to that experienced by their pregnant wives.

The first live elephant was exhibited in the United States in April of 1796.

Lightning has been known to strike the same building several times during a single electrical storm.

Owing to a heavy flow of saliva, a snake's digestion begins immediately and is completed rapidly.

A *martin* is a bird of the swallow family: a *marten* is a fur-bearing animal similar to the weasel.

The Chinese language contains no *r* sound, hence they say "Amelican."

During the American Revolution many patriots melted their pewter to obtain lead for bullets.

Wild ducks and geese are said to do their courting while migrating and are mated and ready to raise families the moment they reach their destination.

A jack rabbit is quickly overtaken by greyhounds, but not by ordinary dogs.

The air space in an egg is never at the small end.

A monarch butterfly may fly almost a thousand miles in search of warmth.

The suction created in a forest fire has been known to be so strong that it has uprooted trees before the flames ever reached them.

There are at least ten species of salmon.

The female swordtail fish has been known to produce as many as one hundred young at birth.

Delaware, Nevada, Vermont, and Wyoming have only one representative in Congress.

An ordinary elm tree of medium size will transpire fifteen thousand pounds of water on a clear, dry, hot day.

The *United States Postal Guide* lists the parishes in Louisiana as "counties."

A ham generally weighs 7 percent of the weight of the live hog.

The state of New York ranks first in popularity among honeymooners. Florida is second.

European vinegar is much milder than American vinegar.

Rabbi Barry Silberg, 32, of Milwaukee, Wisconsin, skipped rope for five hours and completed 43,743 jumps, or 145 per minute.

Three times more women attempt suicide than men.

The cash register was invented by James Ritty, an Ohio saloonkeeper, to keep his bartenders honest.

Leopards are especially fond of the flavor of dog meat.

For 96 out of every 100 American citizens, the right side of their face is more strongly developed than their left.

The little symbol for *and*—&—is the oldest world symbol known and means the same in several hundred languages.

Women in nudist camps tend to wear more makeup than women elsewhere.

John Hancock was the first to sign the Declaration of Independence. Samuel Adams was the second signer.

The anatomy of a frog is such that it must close its eyes to swallow, and if its mouth is held open too long it will suffocate.

Poultrymen are warned against washing eggs before sending them to market.

A goat chews the labels off tin cans in order to get to the paste.

Tidal waves have been known to travel at one thousand miles per hour.

There were three times as many taxicabs in New York City fifty years ago as there are now.

A thoroughbred horse must have a pedigree, but every pedigreed horse is not necessarily a thoroughbred.

Many elephants enjoy chewing tobacco because of the licorice and sugar that it contains.

To serve the 100 senators and 435 representatives in Washington, Congress employs about sixteen thousand people.

In 1882, Henry W. Seely patented the first electric flatiron.

The roots of the dandelion are sometimes used as a substitute for coffee.

The black whip snake is one of the few American snakes that can outrun a man on a poor surface and can run at least as fast as the average man on a good surface.

A goat will nibble at almost anything.

The apparent increase in the size of the sun, moon, and stars when they are near the horizon is chiefly a psychological phenomenon in man.

Historians maintain that the handshake originated in medieval Europe as a gesture between two men to prove they were unarmed.

More than one thousand professional rodeos are held each year in the United States—in all seasons.

Clyde's body was riddled by fifty-four bullets—Bonnie's by fifty.

It's not unusual for some young birds to eat fourteen feet of earthworms per day.

Jealousy in a baby is not recognizable until the age of about twelve months.

Rarely is any woman moved to tears by a melody—but it is not so with men.

Chemists know how, but not why, metal corrodes.

The world uses more than one million tons of chemical pesticides per year.

There are only forty-nine whooping cranes in the United States.

The Soviet Union shares frontiers with thirteen other countries.

Olive oil has been obtained from the fruit of a small tree in the Mediterranean region for more than three thousand years.

The gestation period of a giraffe is from fourteen to fifteen months; a kangaroo requires only thirty-eight to thirty-nine days.

Bank of America is the largest commercial bank in the United States.

The first weightlifting world championship was held in London in 1891.

Spiders are not insects, but they are related to insects.

The first successful steel pen was developed in 1858.

Fifteen percent of all the drivers get seventy-six percent of all the traffic tickets.

Dr. Edward Teller is the father of the hydrogen bomb.

A seven-inch drop can crack a hen's egg.

The longest game of tiddlywinks was played in 1970 by eight Chicago students. The game lasted more than 120 hours.

A hat, last worn by Napoleon in 1815, was sold at a French auction in 1970 for $29,800.

The bar at the Working Men's Club in Mildura, Australia, has a counter 287 feet long, served by thirty-two beer pumps.

To prevent fixing, race horses are identified by numbers tattooed inside their lip.

The oldest working clock, at Salisbury Cathedral in London, was made in 1386.

Bluejays are faster learners than dogs and cats, according to a professor of psychology in Massachusetts.

The game of polo was played in China around the year A.D. 600.

More automobiles are assembled in Kansas City than in any other American city except Detroit.

Gold is seven times as dense as gravel or sand.

After two snails mate, they both lay eggs.

In blackjack, odds generally favor the house by 6 percent.

The water that drains off Japan's Mount Fugi is so polluted with alkaline that negatives can be developed in it.

One certain way to lose weight according to a medical specialist is to wait two minutes between bites.

In Massachusetts it's illegal to shave off your whiskers while driving a car.

Penguins are undoubtedly the dumbest creatures on earth—they aren't afraid of man.

A horse in a burning barn will "freeze," and needs to be blindfolded in order to be led out.

The secret of silk remained inside China for almost nineteen centuries.

The manufacture of one ton of rayon requires three hundred thousand gallons of water.

Salt-water fish are not necessarily saltier than fresh-water fish.

In 1974, the American people used 500 billion matches.

United States currency is engraved on paper made from 100 percent cotton fibers.

Deep water in the summer may have too little oxygen for fish, causing them to come near the water's surface.

The venom of a rattlesnake is worth about thirty-five dollars per milligram. Its meat is worth about four dollars per pound.

In the United States, women make up 53 percent of the electorate.

A first-quarter moon is always a little brighter than a last-quarter moon.

The penalty for stealing in Saudi Arabia is the loss of a hand at the wrist.

Nine out of ten people reported missing turn up of their own accord.

Demosthenes, the ancient Athenian orator, was unable to pronounce the sound expressed by the letter *r*.

When a light bulb is suddenly broken, a popping sound is often produced by the outside air rushing into the near vacuum.

Some wild animals attempt to hide themselves when they feel death approaching. This is especially true of elephants.

Listen to the mockingbird, for it is estimated that it can imitate the song of thirty-two other birds.

A young walrus will eat approximately one hundred pounds of fish daily.

The best selling recording by a female singer was Patti Page's "Tennessee Waltz," in 1950.

An average ebb tide carries one-sixth of the water in San Francisco Bay to the ocean.

If all the razor blades sold in the United States in 1973 could have been stacked on top of one another, the pile would have been more than twenty-thousand feet high.

Some trees live and continue to grow for thousands of years.

The first Olympics was held in 776 B.C.

A labor statistician reports that if a woman is fired or laid off, it's expected she'll be out of work an average of twenty-seven weeks.

Ordinarily, we get just twenty-three minutes and thirty seconds of news on a half-hour television program of network news.

People with type "O" blood live longer—according to a recent research report.

Two out of three wives were acquainted with their husbands for at least two years before they were married.

The Mississippi River carries more than 500 million tons of sediment into the Gulf of Mexico annually.

It seems that rape is the only crime where the victim is expected to prove her own innocence.

The American eel is the only fish that lives and grows in fresh water but spawns in the ocean.

Scientists recently reported that the average person can smell two thousand different odors.

The class ring originated in this country at West Point.

The law in Los Angeles prohibits a woman from hanging out her lingerie in public view.

Eggs that are packed small end down keep better.

On July 24, 1946, the first United States underwater test of the atom bomb was made.

Many years ago the jack rabbit was so named because its large ears were thought to resemble those of a jackass.

Twenty percent of the beer drinkers in the United States drink eighty percent of the beer.

The watermelon originated in Africa.

Vanilla is the most popular ice cream flavor in the United States. Chocolate is second.

The record shows that the average Japanese puts 20 percent of his income into savings.

For four years, from 1875 through 1878, the United States minted a twenty-cent piece.

The Great Pyramid of Egypt contains 2,300,000 limestone blocks. Their average weight is two and one-half tons each.

If you are an adult weighing 175 pounds, in twenty-four hours you will probably speak five thousand words, perspire over one pint, and eat nearly four pounds of food.

Forty percent of what you worry about never happens.

Ten quarts of ice will produce nine quarts of water.

If the larger eggs cost seven cents or more per dozen than the smaller sizes, buy the smaller eggs to save money.

On July 15, 1876, the first no-hit baseball game was pitched by St. Louis' G. W. Bradley against Hartford, Connecticut.

A musical Irishman named Joseph Sweeney invented the banjo.

The Black Plague killed about 25 million people in 1327.

Eight out of every ten marriages are held in church.

The average man's beard has thirteen thousand whiskers.

Despite popular belief, camels can go without water for only two or three days, not one week.

Sand covers less than one-fifth of the vast Sahara Desert.

Corn is not mentioned in the Bible, nor is it mentioned in any other ancient literature of the Old World.

There are Rotary Clubs in 151 countries of the world.

In the United States one automobile may discharge up to one ton of pollutants into the air annually.

Abraham Lincoln was once arrested and charged with "ferrying without a license." He served as his own counsel and was acquitted.

Albania is the only Communist country that has made the practice of religion a punishable crime.

Two and one-half hours is about as long as a woman can play the slot machines at the Nevada clubs when she's in high heels.

The Jewish population of the United States in 1975 was 5,700,000.

A mule deer has been known to jump eight feet from a running start of only a few feet in order to escape a trap.

The suicide rate among female chemists is about two and one-half times as high as among male chemists.

If a queen bee is stolen from a hive, another queen will be found within twelve days.

The teletype was invented in 1928, five years after the television set.

American citizens spend five times as much money annually on dog food as on college textbooks.

Barbed wire was invented in 1874 by an American, Joseph F. Glidden.

Two out of three car buyers pay the asking price without dickering.

The portion of the female anatomy most idealized by the poets is their eyes.

The raccoon likes water and is a strong swimmer.

Atlantic City's famous Boardwalk is five miles long.

No street name in Salt Lake City can be longer than eight letters.

Cellophane was invented by Jacques Edwin Bradenberger in 1908.

Only 12 out of every 100 Italians buy a daily newspaper.

The temperature of any drink has nothing to do with its capacity to quench human thirst.

Bats are the only mammals able to fly.

Only three card games are popular all over the United States: solitaire, poker, and contract bridge.

The average American man will hold down about twelve different full-time jobs in his lifetime.

Full-blooded native Hawaiians account for less than 1 percent of the population of Hawaii.

On July 16, 1945, the first atomic bomb was exploded in New Mexico.

More than one hundred varieties of aspirin are offered for sale in the United States.

The first Mardi Gras parade in New Orleans was held in 1838.

Fish and snakes hear by detecting vibrations from the ground or water.

Ten is that year of life when the average person sees best.

Dogs snap at toads, but do not eat them.

A large part of the natural diet of the channel catfish is insects and their larvae.

It is estimated that there are more than 924 million persons of the Christian faith in the world.

Mud will not stick to diamond.

The largest island on earth is Greenland with an area of 840,000 square miles.

Medical tests indicate that whiskey with soda is more swiftly intoxicating than a like amount of whiskey alone.

Light travels fastest in a vacuum—186,281 miles per second. In air, it's fifty-six miles per second slower.

Wabash, Indiana, was the first city to be lighted by electricity.

Women are more susceptible to diabetes than men.

The common yellow dandelion is a wonder plant —one ounce of this plant provides seven thousand units of vitamin A.

When you flip a penny, it is more likely to come up heads than tails.

The Irish setter now ranks number three on the list of the nation's most popular dogs.

Among single people over forty-five, women make more money than men.

The majority of airline stewardesses come from small towns.

Eighty million Americans are now riding bicycles.

Game experts say that a one-day-old antelope can run up to twenty-three miles per hour.

The South Pole rarely gets more than five inches of new snow in a year.

Almost half of the world's telephones are in the United States.

It has been estimated that each year at least two million Americans are infested with lice.

On September 9, 1836, Abraham Lincoln was licensed to practice law.

The wild turkey is the heaviest land bird in North America.

Ants won't cross a white chalk line.

The official baseball is now covered with cowhide instead of horsehide.

There are an estimated three hundred thousand undomesticated cats in Rome.

The Gateway Arch in St. Louis is 630 feet high.

An elephant seal consumes more than one hundred pounds of food per day.

Ten percent of the United States population lives in a family headed by a woman.

The average dollar bill lasts only about twelve months.

No navy admiral has ever been nominated for the presidency of the United States.

Baltimore was the first city in America to have a street illuminated by gas lights—in 1817.

Most polar bears never set foot on land.

The hardest thing to do in any major sport is to hit a baseball.

A horse or a mule is a backward kicker. A cow is usually a sideways kicker.

Finding fault ranks number one on the list of traits that damage human relationships.

No United States president was an only child.

Italy produces nearly a thousand different types of wine.

In June of 1652, America got its first traffic law.

Almost one out of three households in America has a family dog.

Goat's milk has smaller fat globules, which makes it more digestible than cow's milk.

According to university researchers, people can fall asleep with their eyes open.

The Japanese are the world's top TV watchers.

Americans with some form of religious affiliation make up 62.4 percent of the population.

No coin minted in the United States is officially or legally designated by the term *penny*.

Two times more women use tranquilizers than men according to a recent survey.

The fountain pen was invented by John J. Loud in 1888.

There are no native snakes in Ireland.

Firemen are more subject to heart attack than other men.

Red-haired women almost never become bald.

The word *free* in an advertisement tends to attract the most attention.

Butter can be made from the milk of any mammal.

Salamanders have very slippery skin because of the secretions of many mucous cells.

About a third more plastic surgery is done on the nose in June than in any other month.

Strictly speaking, only the male should be called a *peacock*. The female is properly called a *peahen*. The young are known as *peachicks*.

Despite what is commonly supposed, an electric fan running in a perfectly insulated and hermetically sealed room would not make the air cooler.

A diamond is the only gem composed of only one element.

During June and July in Iceland, daylight is perpetual and a person can read a book by natural light at any time of the "night."

The orange coloring in a prairie dog's eyes permits him to withstand the glare of the sun.

Seven out of every ten houses in the United States are painted white.

The temperature in Caracas, Venezuela, seldom varies more than five degrees during the year.

And/or is a device found in legal and commercial documents and means "either both or only one."

More than 60 million Americans hold credit cards.

The trunk of an elephant contains forty thousand muscles.

Some "beef experts" think that Black Angus meat is better tasting than other beef.

The most powerful man on earth cannot stop a sneeze.

President Andrew Jackson was severely criticized when he bought twenty deluxe spittoons at $12.50 each for the White House.

The highest price ever paid for a tree was the $53,000 spent for a single Starkspur golden delicious apple tree near Yakima, Washington.

Every day twenty pounds of chewing gum is deposited on the bottom of the sixty-two hundred seats at Radio City Music Hall in New York City.

The dental cavities that begin every day outnumber the dentists five to one.

Classical music is played as a background to professional boxing matches in Thailand.

Juvenile records in police departments indicate that girls get tougher sentences than boys. The reverse is true among grownups.

China has more babies under one year old than Australia has people of any age.

The first horse-drawn trolley car was used two thousand years ago in ancient Pompeii. The tracks weren't rails, but grooves in the pavement.

Next to heart disease and cancer, alcoholism is the biggest killer in the United States.

The two steepest streets in the United States are in San Francisco. Filbert Street and 22nd Avenue both have an incline of thirty-three and one-half degrees.

In 1830, the B & O Railroad gave up the horse-pulled locomotive for the steam engine.

Chinese, as officially written in Peking, is a language of more than five thousand different characters.

The fastest of all birds is the peregrine falcon. It has been known to reach a speed of three miles per minute.

On August 12, 1851, Isaac Singer of Pittstown, New York, was granted a patent on his sewing machine.

The longest running show on earth is Ringling Brothers and Barnum and Bailey Circus with more than one hundred years of performances.

Even when blindfolded, some textile experts can tell the dye in a piece of cloth just by touching it.

The shortest English word that contains the first six letters of the alphabet is *feedback*.

One out of four students of karate in this country is a woman.

The average grocery store throws away four garbage cans full of edible food every day.

Approximately 33 out of every 100 husbands can be accurately described as "henpecked."

One inch of rain on one acre of ground would weigh 226,513 pounds and would consist of 27,192 gallons of water.

The latest estimate of bachelor fathers in the United States is 386,000.

As far back as 300 B.C. the Egyptians practiced what we today call hypnotism.

The greater Los Angeles area is eight hundred square miles larger than Rhode Island and Delaware combined.

Some snakes have been known to live for two years without food by absorbing the fat of their own bodies.

The hair of man has more variety of color than the hair of any animal species.

An enormous majority of the seven million horses in this country carry women riders.

The first gold coins were struck in the United States in 1795. The last appeared in 1933.

Lebanon is the only Arab nation without a desert.

Many cows chew on a golf ball as though it were bubblegum.

There are 580 hairs per square inch on the average man's face.

Leaves change color in the autumn due to a decline in the intake of chlorophyll.

Abraham Lincoln walked six miles to school and did his homework on the back of a shovel.

The average American citizen eats twenty-three quarts of ice cream annually.

Big Mike was the largest bear ever killed. His unstretched hide measured twelve feet, four inches wide by ten feet, four inches long.

Seventeen percent of all accidental injuries happen to persons sixty-five and older.

The two nasal cavities on the snout of most fish are pits which function only as sense organs.

At one time in her life, Baby Ruth Pontico achieved fame as the biggest woman in the world. She weighed 815 pounds. Her husband weighed only 130 pounds.

The Cincinnati zoo is the home of the largest number of gorillas born in captivity.

Seven out of ten men who desert their family do so in the first ten years of marriage.

Approximately 45 percent of Americans say they've never traveled more than one hundred miles from their home.

The parrot does not build a nest but lays its eggs in the soft dust that accumulates at the bottom of a decayed tree trunk.

On July 19, 1969, John Fairfax arrived in Florida, becoming the first man to sail across the Atlantic alone.

John S. Temberton, a pharmacist, brewed the first batch of Coca-Cola. The drink was first placed on sale May 8, 1886, for five cents a glass at Jacob's Pharmacy in Atlanta, Georgia.

"The Star Spangled Banner" was officially adopted as the national anthem by Congress on March 3, 1931—117 years after it was composed.

There have been nineteen major civilizations in our world since man first began to form government. Of these nineteen, five still survive.

Only in the elementary school years is the female more likely to tell lies than the male.

It is a matter of record that more pedestrians are killed while crossing *with* the signal than *against* it.

There's not much chalk in chalk. It's mostly plaster of paris.

President Rutherford B. Hayes, who took office in 1877, allowed the first telephone to be installed in the White House.

When a Cape buffalo bull and a lion fight, both usually die.

A violin craftsman often searches through one ton of wood to find a piece good enough to produce a bow weighing less than three ounces.

There are 355,000 lawyers in the United States, but most of them never enter a courtroom.

The earliest reference to rodeo dates back to 1847 in Santa Fe, New Mexico.

Studies show that a goldfish would rather look at a mirror than at another goldfish.

If a human baby grew as fast as a baby whale, it would be about sixty-five feet tall by its second birthday.

In a recent survey, four out of ten wives said they'd marry different husbands if they were to do it all over again.

Only one big league pitcher (Carl Mays) ever killed a batter with a wild pitch. The victim was Ray Chapman of the Cleveland Indians, August 16, 1920.

In towns of population less than five thousand, surveys show that 90 percent of the citizens own a Bible. In larger cities, less than 75 percent own a Bible.

The sassafras or "mitten" tree produces leaves of three or four different patterns, all on the same tree.

It is often asserted that the most aggressive show-business personalities are the offspring of hard-driving mothers.

The world's longest love letter contained 410,000 words.

More than three hundred brands are marketed in the United States.

There is no wood in "petrified wood."

Four people survive out of every seven who go over Niagara Falls in a barrel.

The steps to the United States Capitol number exactly 365, one for each day of the year.

About 44 percent of all murders are committed with handguns.

A newborn baby will keep its fists tightly clenched for the first two weeks of its life.

There are comparatively few double beds in Norway.

Egyptian vultures can break ostrich eggs by striking the shell with a rock held in their beak.

In 1843, an ordinance was passed in Philadelphia prohibiting bathing from November 1 to March 1.

Grover Jones and his wife, of Peterson, West Virginia, had fifteen sons.

It is proper and official to call Icelanders by their first name only.

Some flowers that appear red to human beings are black to bees.

An average of 102 tornadoes touch down annually in Texas.

If you want perfume to last all evening, apply it right after drying off from a hot bath.

Aspirin makers claim that the average American grownup has fifty headaches per year.

In 1790, the national debt per person was $19.56. Today it is more than $2,046.00 per person.

Fifteen million adults in the United States are over fifty-five.

Statistically, California is the most dangerous state in which to drive a car. Texas comes in second.

It's said that only three husbands out of five know the color of their wife's eyes.

The origin of the phrase "to face the music" goes back to 1785.

Some drunken drivers in South Africa are given jail sentences as long as ten years.

The bodies of at least eighteen Americans have been preserved in cold storage after death.

Our digestive system works better when we sleep on our right side—according to the medical experts.

Horses breathe only through their nostrils.

The customary Christmas Eve dish in Italy is roast eel.

American couples living in "unwedded bliss" skyrocketed by more than 700 percent from 1960 to 1970.

The earliest known encyclopedia was compiled by Speusippus, a nephew of Plato, in Athens, in 370 B.C.

More than forty diseases in the United States can be transmitted from dog to man.

Eskimo children are customarily permitted to play with very sharp knives.

Protestant female missionaries outnumber Protestant male missionaries three to two.

The prostate is the second most frequent site of cancer in men.

Citation was the first race horse to win one million dollars—in 1951.

The female mosquito can live on plant juices, but she prefers blood.

In 1795, Francois Appert, a Frenchman, devised a way to preserve food in sealed glass jars.

It now costs the Bureau of Engraving and Printing eleven dollars to turn out one thousand bills of any denomination.

The first nightclub in the world was opened in Paris, in 1843.

A human mother outweighs her child by about sixteen to one.

The apple and the rose are distant cousins.

California is the only state in the Union that grows almonds.

A giraffe's tongue is so long that it is used to clean the ears.

Mildred ranks number nine among the most widely used names for women. Number nine for the men is *Frank*.

Americans consume approximately 63 billion eggs per year.

Birds with a vocabulary of at least one hundred words are fairly common.

Ben Foulds, 28, retained his title as Great Britain's pipesmoking champion and won a $2,480 prize by keeping one pipeful of tobacco going for 121 minutes and 16 seconds.

With 120,000 new cases each year, skin cancer is the most prevalent malady in the United States.

A sheet of 100 percent cotton-fiber writing paper can be folded more than one thousand times without breaking.

Some three hundred thousand New Yorkers walk to work every day.

Up to the year 1975, only twenty-four FBI agents have been killed in the line of duty.

Eight presidents and three vice presidents of the United States were from Ohio.

A wood block one inch square and two and one-half inches deep can support ten thousand pounds—the approximate weight of three automobiles.

In 1882, Congress chose the bald eagle as the national emblem.

Monkeys are becoming less hairy from generation to generation.

Nobody has ever made a paint that's perfectly black or perfectly white.

The United States now has almost eight thousand hospitals—more than any other nation in the world.

It is estimated that about half of all divorced citizens are the offspring of divorced parents.

The antelope has only two toes on each foot—instead of the four found on most hoofed animals.

Canada does not have an official national anthem.

The silk in a spider's web is one of the strongest materials known, having tensile strength greater than steel.

Senator William Proxmire of Wisconsin can read material such as the Congressional Record at the rate of about one thousand words per minute.

The first Jewish community was established in North America in 1654.

A construction authority says that the Great Pyramid in the Egyptian desert would cost $1.12 billion were it to be built today.

Only 2 or 3 percent of all children are born with a congenital deformity.

A full-grown black bear usually weighs from 250 to 300 pounds, but its newborn cubs may tip the scales at less than a pound, sometimes weighing only eight ounces.

Mrs. Richard M. Nixon traveled 131,723 miles during her husband's occupancy of the White House.

Women have a harder time than men telling left from right.

The average single woman puts in more years on the job than the average man. She can expect to work forty-five years, he only forty-three.

Crib death kills eight thousand infants each year in the United States.

The guitar is unquestionably the world's most popular musical instrument.

In the cow, only the nose has sweat glands.

The first man to sugar-coat pills was a Philadelphia druggist named William R. Warner—in 1856.

There are 170 nations deeply in debt to the United States. The sum due our government from those far-flung countries runs to more than $51 billion.

A noted horseman in Kentucky contends that almost all horses are southpaws.

Oysters can change their sex.

Men are better than women at judging distance.

The nation's leader in gold production is the state of South Dakota with the Homestake Mine in

Lawrence County the largest mine in the United States.

About one-third of the households in the United States have a dishwasher.

Honey is the sugar handled best by the kidneys.

Far more girls than boys leave the farm as soon as they become old enough.

Next to oil, coffee is the most valuable product in world trade.

The 4-H Club originated in Holmes County, Mississippi, in 1907, as a series of "corn clubs" for boys.

By the time it is three weeks old a baby bat is usually out every night hunting its own food.

Twice as many people are injured at home as at their place of employment.

The first traffic control system was put in use in 1915.

Snapping turtles never feed out of water because they cannot swallow unless their head is submerged.

The first televised prize fight was the bout between Lou Nova and Max Baer—in 1939. Nova won by a knockout in the first round.

Each year about twenty thousand Americans suffer from amnesia.

It takes three times as much energy to toast bread in an oven as in a pop-up toaster.

When frightened or in danger, the yellowfin grouper, a black fish, instantly changes its color to blend with the surroundings.

It is claimed that there are now 250,000 women in the United States who are confirmed pipe smokers.

Statistically, the age at which a man is most likely to buy his first home is thirty-four.

Three out of every ten shotgun shells are fired at rabbits.

About 350,000 babies will be born in the next twenty-four hours.

The world's largest frogs are believed to be those found in the Montaro river in Peru. They measure as much as twenty-four inches in length.

The disease that is said to be most feared by women is breast cancer. By men, heart attacks.

Animal acts are banned from the Miss America Pageant.

The width of a tornado averages between three and four hundred yards, but some have been as narrow as nine feet.

Of the sixty basic appliances now on the market, only ten were generally available back in the 1920s.

The penal code in Lebanon permits a man to execute the wife, sister, mother, or daughter whose sexual promiscuity shames the family.

Every fifteen seconds, somewhere in this country an automobile crashes.

The favorite sport in the Philippines is cock fighting. Every village has a pit.

Columbia University researchers report that they've proved that men are inclined to get angry at *things* while women are more apt to get angry at *people*.

The average length of the honeymoon for first-time brides is nine days.

Bluefin tuna, caught off the coast of Newfoundland, weigh up to eight hundred pounds.

Half the men and women who go into sales jobs either quit or get fired within two years.

The first gun fired in the Revolutionary War was a pistol—at Lexington, Massachusetts, in 1775.

Most of the people in India who are attacked by crocodiles are first bitten on the behind.

A herd of zebras never all sleep at the same time.

Census surveys show that seven out of every ten wives between the ages of eighteen and twenty-four expect to have no more than two children.

The Chinese were playing the harmonica as far back as twenty-six hundred years before Christ.

Most people spend no more than eleven minutes at a time in unbroken, motionless slumber.

The unmarried girl under twenty-one is statistically most inclined to get a headache.

Eighty-two percent of all American husbands think their wives are more attractive now than on their wedding day.

An elm tree planted by Daniel Webster's father seventeen years before the birth of his famous son still shades the log cabin in Franklin, New Hampshire, where this son was born in 1782.

Only about one woman in fifty can stand on her head without help.

Australia is the only continent in the world that contains only one country.

Only once has the United States ever had three presidents in one year: in 1841 Martin Van Buren, William Henry Harrison, and John Tyler each served as president.

The greatest recorded distance for throwing a standard five-pound brick is 135 feet, 8 inches, by Robert Gardner of Gloucestershire, England, in 1970.

Daniel Webster originated the practice of standing when the national anthem is sung or played.

The typewriter was invented before the fountain pen.

Alcohol and related problems cost the United States more than $25 billion per year.

At the age of twenty-two, Stephen Foster wrote the song "Oh Susannah" and become famous overnight.

The most popular Christmas card is the Madonna and Child.

Almost half of child poisonings involve aspirin.

When elephants bathe, they like to squirt water over themselves.

Tailors of old nourished the superstition that any material cut on Friday couldn't be sewn to fit properly.

The earthquake that hit Charleston, South Carolina, on August 31, 1886, damaged three-quarters of the city's buildings.

Men don't faint—they black out. Women faint.

The first silk stockings ever made were a gift to Queen Elizabeth I.

Paper towels were first marketed in 1907.

A blind dog in Eureka, Kansas, is guided by the family's two cats as it walks.

James Monroe was the last United States president to wear knee trousers.

Women tend to be more satisfied with their first name than men.

The outer skin of a hot dog is made from wood cellulose.

On November 18, 1883, the United States was divided into four time zones and standard time was adopted throughout the country.

The kind of fur most preferred by American women seems to be Persian lamb.

Experts think the biggest of the blue whales weigh up to 170 tons.

The longest crawl (on hands and feet) on record is 5.53 miles in nine hours, sixteen minutes by Morgan Remil, 38, of Denmark.

Of the 103 Veteran's Administration cemeteries in the United States, 47 are completely full.

The male mosquito goes on growing as long as he lives.

Lightning strikes the earth somewhere one hundred times each second.

There are twenty-eight thousand veterinarians in the United States.

Librarians in Lufkin, Texas, report that objects

found in returned books include a piece of bacon, a sock, and one-half of a peanut butter sandwich.

On November 8, 1950, the first battle between jet aircraft took place as North Korean and United States planes crashed.

It has been proven that more men than women cry at the movies.

A mature leaf-eating caterpillar can eat an entire square-foot leaf in twenty-four hours.

The worst yellow fever epidemic in Louisiana's history killed eleven thousand people in New Orleans in 1853.

It's against the law to make a pastry reproduction of the White House.

The country with the highest rate of heart attack is Finland.

Women between twenty and thirty are the best secret-keepers.

Many contend that no meat on earth has a richer and more delicious flavor than cougar steak.

Approximately 33 percent of the telephone numbers in Los Angeles are unlisted.

Mahogany trees are cut at night because the tree is more free of sap, more sound, and of richer color.

The shadow reported to be the longest in the world stretches more than two hundred miles off the Canary Islands. The shadow is cast by El Tition Peak.

Recent studies indicate that there are more women that love two men than men who love two women.

Relative to a bird's overall size, its brain is enormous.

It costs the United States Census Bureau $1.22 per person to count Americans.

Two sociologists report that if a girl is the youngest in her family, she's a poorer marriage risk than her older sisters.

Oklahoma legislators once passed a law which prohibited catching of whales in that state.

Twin beds were originally created for use in only extremely hot weather.

The minute hand on Big Ben in London is eleven feet long.

For many years it was traditional among Chinese who wore eyeglasses to remove them when talking to superiors.

On November 1, 1952, the United States exploded the first hydrogen bomb at the Eniwetok atoll in the Marshall Islands.

The moon has less than one-third of the amount of gold found in the earth.

About 12 million American families move every year.

There are sixteen different ways to tie a cravat.

The Indian elephant is a first-class working animal of even temper. It requires a great deal of food—about two hundred pounds per day.

Approximately 123 million people are licensed to drive on United States highways.

Sleep researchers contend it takes about seven minutes for the average American to doze off each night.

More than one-fourth of all divorces occur sometime during the first three years of marriage.

The average Oriental rug will last from thirty to sixty years.

Fourteen percent of the human brain and spinal column is pure cholesterol.

Count on one quart of ice cream yielding six to eight servings.

Rome is nearer the North Pole than New York City.

When they are working, the sled dogs of polar Eskimos are fed only every other day.

In Ancient China, a man could divorce his wife if she talked too much.

More Humor Books from SIGNET

☐ **BUMPER SNICKERS by Bill Hoest.** (#Q7128—95¢)

☐ **FUNNY FIZZLES by Bill Nellor and Jim Molica.**
(#Y7973—$1.25)

☐ **THE VIRTUE OF VERA VALIANT by Stan Lee and Frank Springer.** (#Y7526—$1.25)

☐ **THE VIRTUE OF VERA VALIANT #2 by Stan Lee and Frank Springer.** (#Y7699—$1.25)

☐ **HIP KIDS' LETTERS FROM CAMP by Bill Adler.**
(#Q7107—95¢)

☐ **MORE LETTERS FROM CAMP by Bill Adler.**
(#Q7105—95¢)

☐ **STILL MORE LETTERS FROM CAMP by Bill Adler.**
(#Q7106—95¢)

☐ **SUPERFAN by Nick Meglin and Jack Davis.**
(#Q6302—95¢)

☐ **SUPERFAN . . . AGAIN! by Nick Meglin and Jack Davis.**
(#Q6038—95¢)

☐ **SCROOGIE by Tug McGraw and Mike Witte.**
(#Q6961—95¢)

☐ **SCROOGIE #2: HELLO THERE, BALL! by Tug McGraw and Mike Witte.** (#Y7521—$1.25)

☐ **WEE PALS: NIPPER AND NIPPER'S SECRET POWER by Morrie Turner.** (#T5990—75¢)

☐ **TV OR NOT TV: An Irreverent Look at Television by Bart Andrews and Judy Ervin.** (#Y7660—$1.25)

☐ **IT'S HARD TO BE HIP OVER THIRTY by Judith Viorst.**
(#Y4124—$1.25)

☐ **PEOPLE AND OTHER AGGRAVATIONS by Judith Viorst.**
(#Y5016—$1.25)

THE NEW AMERICAN LIBRARY, INC.,
P.O. Box 999, Bergenfield, New Jersey 07621

Please send me the books I have checked above. I am enclosing
$_____ (check or money order—no currency or C.O.D.'s).
Prices and numbers are subject to change without notice. Please
include the list price plus the following amounts for postage and
handling: 35¢ for Signets, Signet Classics, and Mentors; 50¢ for
Plumes, Meridians, and Abrams.

Name_____

Address_____

City_____State_____Zip Code_____
Allow at least 4 weeks for delivery